ESL For Teachers

Business English in the Classroom

Alycia C. Jones

Why did I write this book?

I have been teaching English for 15 years. In 2008 I founded my own company, ASAP Coaching, a training consultancy which provides business English courses for adults in a wide range of businesses in France.

When I started looking for material to use with my trainees, I found a huge variety of books on the market. I bought and used several, but I consistently found that it made more sense to use a combination of material from these different books to teach rather than one book in particular.

This prompted me to put my ideas on paper with the objective of having everything I wanted in one book.

After years of teaching, I have figured out what works and what doesn't.

In this book, I have mapped out a series of business lessons that focus on the key vocabulary for the business world and that review the essential grammatical structures.

Each unit provides a combination of methods including brainstorming, pair work, small and big group discussions, listening and presentations, among others. The chapters provide you with a theme and some structured activities, but they leave you the freedom to organize things the way you want.

The lessons are helpful when you are having a difficult time coming up with content for a class. They are also useful when you are in a rush and you don't have time to prepare a lesson!

Why should you read this book?

Do you teach English to students or adults who are preparing to work in the business world?

Do you find yourself constantly looking for new material to use in class?

Are you a busy individual with a lot on your plate? If you answered yes to any of these questions, this book is for you.

With twelve complete lessons based on a variety of pertinent business topics, this book will provide you with the material you need to teach an interesting and lively class, as well as the resources a business person needs to survive in the business world!

About the author

Alycia C. Jones was born in San Francisco. Living in France for more than 15 years now, she teaches English with passion in schools and companies.

In 2007, she created the company ASAP Coaching (www.asap-coaching.com) and started to imagine her first educational material.

In 2011, she created www.asap-videos.com, a website about learning English with videos.

In 2014, she created a series of educational books focusing on Business English.
This book is one of them.

Special Amazon bonus

We've reserved a special bonus for Amazon readers; it's a **great** offer for our other books, **Business English in 5 minutes, Speak fluent English** (like a native) and **ESL for Teachers** :

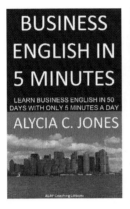 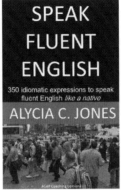 

Business English in 5 minutes, Speak Fluent English and **Fuel for lively conversations in English** are excellent add-ons to **ESL for Teachers.**

And you can actually get one of them for free!

Please find their description and what it's all about here on this private page of our website :

http://www.asap-videos.com/amazon-bonus

Detailed Table of contents

Chapter 1 – A company (Lesson 1)

1. Introduction

In this section, you will cover the various aspects of a company, looking at:
- The organization of a company, including all the different departments and their roles

- The links between each department and how they relate to one another

- The business activities a company can engage in (products or services)

In terms of grammar and vocabulary, you will review:
- The present simple to talk about company organization

- Vocabulary related to a company

2. Brainstorming: Company Departments

Have a brainstorming session to elicit the names of the different departments and managers within a company. You should aim to have the following departments on the board:
- Finance/accounting
- Purchasing
- Sales
- Research and development
- Production
- Human resources
- IT
- Reception/Administration
- Marketing / Advertising / Communications
- Logistics/Supply chain
- Import / Export
- Health and safety
- Quality
- Customer service.

There will likely also be :
- CEO
- Management
- Board of directors
- Shareholders / stockholders

etc. for the key stakeholders / managers.

If the students don't come up with some of the above items, ask them some questions to guide them.

3. Grammar Review: Present Simple

Review of the present simple. Remind the students that they use the present simple to speak about every-day activities and general facts. When they describe the activities of each department and manager, they should always use the present simple, not the present continuous.

4. Small Group Discussion: Department Responsibilities

Break the class into groups of 3 or 4 and have them discuss the following questions:
1. What does the finance department do? Why is this department important to a company?

2. What is the research and development department responsible for? What kinds of problems do you imagine this department faces?

3. How does the purchasing department operate? Who do they purchase goods from? (suppliers)

4. What makes a good sales representative? What is the ultimate goal of the sales department?

5. How does the marketing department operate? What kind of techniques do they use?

6. What is advertising and why is it important?

7. What is the role of the communications department / section? Speak about both internal and external communication.

8. What does the logistics / supply chain department do? What challenges can they have in doing their work?

9. What do import and export departments need to know when doing business with other countries? (customs legislation, foreign regulations, etc.)

10. What is the role of the health and safety department? What kinds of risks do they work against?

11. What is the quality department responsible for? How do they do this?

12. What is the role of the customer service department?

13. What does the CEO do? (runs the company)

14. What is the board of directors? (group composed of elected members who make decisions about company policy)

15. What are shareholders / stockholders? (groups or individuals who own shares in a company, which makes them partial owners of the company)

5. Pair Work: Organizational Chart

Have them work in pairs and organize the brainstormed departments into an organizational chart for a fictitious company or for their own company, if they work for one.

For each department, have them summarize the roles and tasks of the department. They should also consider the links each department has with the other departments in the company. Share these ideas as a big group.

For the links between the departments, some have more important connections than others.
For example the health and safety department has a strong link with the production department, because the biggest hazards occur on the production line during working hours.

Logistics / supply chain has a very strong link with the IT department, because nowadays all products that are shipped out of a company have computerized bar codes for traceability.

The students may not come up with all the links, but the idea with this discussion is to get them thinking about who works with whom and who counts on whom to get their jobs done. If the students have a hard time coming up with the links, give them the above examples.

6. Group Discussion: Company Objectives

Why do companies exist? (to earn money, of course) What activities do companies do? Elicit the different types of activities a company can do. The students should come up with two main ideas for this: to sell products or to offer services. During the next part of the discussion, focus on both these ideas one at a time.

1. Where do a company's products come from? (They can manufacture the products themselves or buy them from suppliers)

2. When a company manufactures its own products, what kinds of things do they need to take into consideration? (purchase of raw materials, adequate factory space and production lines, etc.)

3. When a company buys from a supplier, what do they need to take into consideration? (the good standing of the supplier, the quality of the products bought, the timing for manufacturing the products and delivering them on time, etc.)

4. What kind of services can a company offer? (Internet, mobile phone, cable, etc.)

5. What kinds of problems can a service company have? (technical problems that make it impossible to delivery their service in a timely or correct manner, for example)

7. Listening: A New Employee

Company Life (audio files found on the ASAP Coaching video site; see link at the back of the book in the bonus section to have access).

Transcript:
Amy Anderson is the recruitment officer of Keller & Langston, an international company that produces baby food. She is taking Greg Heller, a new employee in the Supply Chain Department on a tour of the company.

- First let me show you the main offices. Then we will head back to the warehouse and the area where the supply chain department is located.
- It's much bigger than I expected.
- People are often surprised, but we have more than 100 employees on site here. This is the purchasing department. You will be working closely with them for the purchase of the raw materials. Between them and the import and export folks, they will be your key contacts here.
- IT too, I suppose.
- Of course. They are on the second floor. I will introduce you to Jake, who is the one you need to contact in case of problems.
- What about production? I will need to have a contact in the plant, too.
- Before we go to the warehouse, let's go through the factory so I can introduce you to Tom, the line manager. You will also be working closely with him to make sure the products are ready for shipment on time.
- What's on the first floor?
- Let's see. R&D, health and safety, finance and HR. HR is probably the most important for you.
- And finance—especially if they are responsible for paying me!

- In fact, the pay officer works in the HR department, not the finance department. They take care of the budget, taxes and bigger administrative tasks.
- Good to know.

8. Homework

Tell the students to study the vocabulary related to the organization of a company for the next lesson. They should know the names of all the departments and what they are each responsible for.

9. Vocabulary Bank

Departments:
- **Finance**: manages the company's money and is responsible for the financial statements
- **Accounting**: deals with the money coming in and out of a company; often part of the finance department
- **Purchasing**: responsible for buying everything a company needs to operate
- **Sales**: in charge of selling the company's products
- **Research and Development**: finds new ideas and innovation for future products
- **Production**: manufactures the products the company sells
- **Human Resources**: responsible for hiring, firing, payroll, benefits, training and staff well-being
- **IT**: manages computer networks
- **Reception/Admin.**: welcomes people, deals with the mail and phone calls
- **Marketing**: responsible for selling and promoting a company's products
- **Advertising**: in charge of attracting customers to buy products
- **Communications**: deals with internal and external communication, including PR (public relations)
- **Logistics**: manages the receipt, storage and shipment of all the goods that move in and out of a company
- **Supply Chain**: manages all products a company deals with from raw materials (point of origin) to the end-user (point of sale); linked to the logistics department
- **Import**: manages the products that are purchased from abroad and shipped to the company (raw materials)
- **Export**: manages the products that are produced at the company and shipped abroad (finished goods)

- **Health and Safety**: responsible for enforcing safe working conditions for all staff and taking preventative measures against any hazards
- **Quality**: checks the quality of the goods that a company sells
- **Customer Service**: deals with customer complaints and problems

Other related vocabulary:
- **CEO**: person who runs the company
- **Management**: group of managers who are responsible for the various departments in the company
- **Board of Directors**: group composed of elected members who make decisions about company policy
- **Shareholders / stockholders**: groups or individuals who own shares in a company, which makes them partial owners of the company
- **Stakeholders**: the people who have an interest in a company (shareholders, management, employees, etc.)
- **Suppliers**: a company that sells goods or services to a retail company, which then sells the products in their stores

Chapter 2 - A company (Lesson 2)

1. Introduction

In this section you will look at:
- Sectors companies can be involved in

- Competition

In terms of grammar and vocabulary, you will review:
- The present continuous to talk about company performance

- The future with "will" to make predictions about the future

- Vocabulary related to business sectors

- Vocabulary related to competition

2. Review of the Previous Lesson

Take some time to review what you did during the last lesson. Have the students remind you about the names of each of the departments in a company and what they do. You can do this orally or you can write 10 words on the board at random and have them do a pop quiz during which they have to write definitions in English for the selected words.

3. Brainstorming: Job Sectors

Tell the students you are going to speak about the different sectors in the business world. Have them guess as many as they can and get them up on the board. The following is an incomplete list of sectors, including the most important ones. They may come up with others. Have them try to name a company for each sector:
- Automotive / aerospace (GM, Ford, Volkswagen, Toyota, Boeing, Airbus...)

- Banking and finance (Bank of America, HSBC, JP Morgan Chase, Citigroup...)

- Chemistry and pharmaceuticals (Bausch & Lomb, Johnson & Johnson, Aventis...)

- Consumer goods / retail (Procter and Gamble, Amazon, Walmart...)

- Food and drink industry (Coca-Cola, Pepsico, Danone, Mars...)

- Health (3M, Kaiser Permanente...)

- Insurance (AAA, Allstate, Farmers...)

- Manufacturing (GE, Samsung, Apple, IBM...)

- Mining industry (Vale, Rio Tinto...)

- Public sector (government employees, also called civil servants or public servants)

- Telecommunications (AT&T, T-Mobile, Orange...)

- Tourism (Lonely Planet, Air Asia, Hyatt...)

- Transportation / logistics (Amtrak Express, United Airlines, The UPS Store...)

- Utilities and energy (PG&E, Edison International...)
etc.

4. Grammar Review: Present Continuous

Review of present continuous. Remind the students they use this tense to talk about something that is happening at the moment or in the near future. Put the structure on the board if there are any doubts.

5. Small Group Discussion Questions: Sector Performance

1. Which of the sectors mentioned above are doing well?

2. Which ones are doing poorly?

3. Why are they performing well / badly?

4. Which sectors are having a positive / negative influence on the economy?

5. What companies are doing well this year?

6. Which ones are not doing well?

7. Which countries' economies are doing well?

6. Grammar Review Part 2: The Future Using "Will"

For this exercise, you may want to remind them of the structure of the future and the use of "will" when making predictions for the future.

7. Group Discussion: Predictions about the Future of Business

- What is the future of the sectors mentioned above?

- Which sectors do you think will thrive in the future? Which ones will fail?

- Have the students work in pairs to make their evaluation of the future of business. After they have spoken with their partner, have the groups share their forecasts with the rest of the class.

8. Interaction: Brand Competitors

Write the word "competition" on the board and ask the students if they know what it means. Have them give you examples of competition.

Competitors: Talk about the following competitors. Which is more powerful or well-known? What is the public opinion about the companies? Which has the stronger sense of competition? Why?
- McDonalds and Burger King

- Coca Cola and Pepsi

- Toyota and Honda

- Apple iPhone and Samsung Galaxy

- Zara and H&M

- Amazon and eBay

- Facebook and Twitter

9. Pair Work: Competition

Have the students work in pairs to speak about the following questions:

1. Are you a competitive person? Are you a poor sport when you lose?

2. Do you think it is good for schools to encourage a competitive spirit among students? Why? Why not?

3. Why do you think of competition between co-workers in the workplace? Is this a good way to motivate staff? Can it be bad?

4. What do you think about competition between companies? Is this an inevitable part of the business world?

5. Which industries have the toughest competitors? Why?

6. What is industrial espionage?

7. How do companies "spy" on each other? Is this illegal? Unethical? Normal?

8. Do you think it is wrong for a company to collect data about a competitor? Why? Why not?

10. Role Play: Competitive Intelligence

Break the class into pairs and have them prepare the following competition role play.

- Scenario 1 (Student A)
You have been hired by Organic Star to work in the competitive intelligence section of the IT department. From what you understood during the job interview, your main task will be collecting data about Organic Star's competitors. You will need to gather information about the company, its customers and its products, analyze the information and compile it into a report to share with the management. The idea is, the better you know your competition, the more effectively you can work. Before coming to work at Organic Star, you worked at Lil' Orchard, one of Organic Star's biggest competitors. When you accepted the new job, you made it quite clear that you had signed a non-competition clause with Lil' Orchard, and you had no intention of revealing any information that was not already readily available to the public. You are having a meeting with your boss to speak about this project.

- Scenario 2 (Student B)
You are the manager of the competitive intelligence section, and you want your new employee to speak to you about the recipes for Lil' Orchard's famous Strawberry Swirl Custard and its line of fresh dairy desserts, which is number one on the market. You know that if you can learn the details of the recipe, Organic Star can win some much-needed market share and have more competitive advantage on the market. Try to convince your employee to talk to you.

11. Listening: Corporate Espionage

Competition (audio files found on the ASAP Coaching video site; see link at the back of the book in the bonus section to have access).

Transcript: Mike Jackson is the competitive intelligence manager at Organic Star. He is speaking to Gretchen Smith, his new employee about her former employer, Lil' Orchard.

- How long were you there?
- Almost three years.
- Long enough to get the lay of the land, I'd say.
- Sure. It's not a very big company.
- Yet they dominate the market for organic dairy desserts. They are our biggest rival.
- Mike, you're fishing. You know as well as I do that I am not going to tell you anything confidential.
- I am not asking you to reveal state secrets. In fact, I am not asking you to reveal anything. But if I should happen to stumble onto some information, I would just like confirmation, that's all.
- Is that why you hired me?
- Not at all! We hired you because you're good.
- Tell me something, Mike. How would you react if you discovered that I was sharing Organic Star's secrets with a competitor? You would fire me, right?
- Hmmm. Probably.
- So don't ask me to do something that you wouldn't want me to do if the tables were turned.
- Just one question. For the Strawberry Swirl Custard, is it vanilla extract or powdered vanilla?
- Mike!
- All right! All right! But I am convinced there's something about the vanilla.

- No comment.

Discussion:
- What are the ethical issues raised by this conversation?
- What obligation does Gretchen have towards her former company? Towards her new company?
- Should a company expect employees to reveal confidential information about former employers?
- What is a non-competition clause and what role does it play in situations like the one above?

12. Homework

Tell the students to study the vocabulary related to the various job sectors and competition for the next lesson.

13. Vocabulary Bank

Job sectors:
- **Automotive**: manufactures cars, trucks, etc.
- **Aerospace**: designs and manufactures aircraft (and missiles, spacecraft, etc.)
- **Banking/Finance**: banks and financial institutions that lend money and assist clients with investments
- **Food and drink**: produces all food and beverages for public consumption
- **Chemistry/Pharmaceuticals**: research, create, develop and sell drugs for medical use
- **Consumer goods/retail**: manufactures goods for mass consumption, including food, clothing, electronics, etc.
- **Health**: offers medical services through hospitals, HMOs (health maintenance organizations) and medical products
- **Manufacturing**: transformation of mechanical, chemical or physical components into finished goods (cars, textiles, etc.)
- **Mining**: extracting minerals from the earth
- **Public sector**: those employees who hold government jobs
- **Telecommunications**: includes network operators, service providers, manufacturers of cell phones, etc.
- **Tourism**: services for people who wish to travel by sea, train, air, etc.
- **Transportation/Logistics**: responsible for transporting goods and people (trucking companies, railroads, airlines, etc.)
- **Utilities**: providers of electric, gas and water for public consumption

Vocabulary related to competition:
- **To compete**: to work against another party or company, especially for profit when related to business
- **Competitor**: company or person than is in competition; a rival
- **Competitive**: a strong need or desire to succeed or perform better than someone else
- **Market share**: percentage of sales a specific product has on the market for a given period of time
- **Rival**: competitor
- **To dominate**: to control (A top competitor dominates the market.)

Chapter 3 - Communication (Lesson 1)

1. Introduction

In this section you will look at:
- Forms of communication (written and verbal)

- How to telephone in English

In terms of grammar and vocabulary, you will review:
- The past simple to speak about communication in the past

- The comparative and the superlative to compare communication in the past and communication today

- Typical telephone vocabulary

2. Review of the previous lesson

Take some time to review what was done during the last two lessons. Quickly go over the competition and job sector vocabulary, as well as the vocabulary for the various departments for a company. You may want to give a pop quiz at the beginning of the class or just an oral review to make sure the vocabulary has been revised.

3. Brainstorming: Communication

Write "Communication" on the board, and have the students brainstorm. Don't give them any direction or indication of what the subject will be. Just see what ideas they get on the board.

Tell them you are first going to focus on ways to communicate: written and verbal. Later in the lesson you will look at the methods that are used to be an effective communicator.

4. Grammar Review: Comparatives and Superlatives

Review of comparative and superlative and past simple. The students should be familiar with these structures, but if they are not, take a few minutes to write some examples on the board and go over them. For the past simple, remind them of the list of irregular verbs that they may need to revise if they are rusty.

5. Small Group Discussion: The Evolution of Communication

Have the students work in small groups to discuss the following topic and then share their ideas as a big group.

Compare communication in the past and communication in the present. Here are some things to consider during the conversation: communication between family members, friends, co-workers, neighbors, strangers; the role of technology in the evolution of communication (telephones, cell phones, smart phones, computers, tablets, etc.); conflict management and dealing with difficult situations; the work place: how has communication changed for the different sectors you spoke about in lesson 2? Have the changes in technology in the communication sector been beneficial to us? In what ways? In what ways have those changes been detrimental?

6. Pair work: Means of Communication

1. How many forms of communication can you name?

2. What forms of written communication do you use most frequently?

3. How many emails, texts, tweets, etc. do you send per day? What are the subjects of these messages?

4. How much time do you spend on the phone per day?

5. Do you like/dislike talking on the phone? Why?

6. Do you prefer emailing someone, phoning or meeting face to face? What are the advantages and disadvantages of these three forms of communication?

7. How is communication between people changing today?

7. Group Discussion: Telephone

Telephone: See what vocabulary the students know by asking the following questions:
- What is the word for pushing the numbers on the phone? (to dial)

- What sound does the phone make? (ring)

- What do you do when the phone rings? (you answer)

- What do you do when you are finished with the call? (you hang up)

- When the person you are calling is already on the phone, you say the line is (busy: US; engaged: UK).

- If the person you want to speak to is not available and you want him to call you back, what do you do? (leave a message)

- If you plan to phone to a person at a later time, what are you going to do? (to call back)

- When you give your name letter by letter, what do you do? (spell your name)

- What can you say if you don't understand? (I'm sorry, I didn't catch that. Can you repeat, please?)

- What do you say if the person you are speaking to is speaking too fast? (Could you please speak more slowly? Can you slow down, please?)

Discuss:

a. Have you ever had to phone someone in English?

b. What kind of difficulties can you have when calling someone in English?

c. How do you prepare for a phone call in English?

d. What's your best/worst experience phoning someone in English?

e. If you have to deal with a problem in English, would you rather do it by phone or by e-mail.

8. Role play: Phoning Practice

Have your students do one or all of the following phone role plays to practice phoning.

- Scenario 1 (Student A):
You would like to reserve a plane ticket from London to New York, round trip. You would like to leave on April 3 and return on April 12. These dates are flexible, but only by 1 or 2 days (you can leave one or two days before or after, but not more than that). You want to be in New York for 8 full days. Your budget is 400 euros. Be sure to request the seating arrangement you would like (aisle or window). Be ready to spell your name. You credit card number is 8394 5934 9820 0012. The expiration date is 08/15.

- Scenario 1 (Student B):
You work for British Airways. Someone will call to reserve a flight with you. The only dates available for the flight are from April 1 to April 10. The cost of this flight is 450 euros. If the person decides to reserve, be sure to ask his/her name, credit card number and the expiration date of the card.

- Scenario 2 (Student A):
You are going on holiday to San Francisco. You hotel is included in the price of your plane ticket, but you would like some additional excursions. Call a travel agency to make the following arrangements:
A rental car for five days from 01/08 to 06/08, two reservations for Alcatraz Island on 07/08, a day trip to the Napa Valley to go wine-tasting on 09/08, reservations for two at Millennium, one of San Francisco's top restaurants, on 05/08 at 8pm.

- Scenario 2 (Student B):

You work for San Francisco Bay Travel Agency. A customer will call you to reserve some excursions. Ask for the dates and give the prices. A rental car is $30 per day from a compact car, $50 per day for a mid-size car and $100 per day for an SUV. Tickets for Alcatraz Island are $25 each. On 07/08, the tours are fully booked so there is no possibility to go to Alcatraz. However, there are some tickets at 2pm and 4pm on 08/08. A trip to Napa Valley is $150 per person for a full day tour, including wine-tasting in 5 wineries and a picnic. Millennium Restaurant has no tables available at 8pm on 05/08, but there is a possibility at 6pm.

- Scenario 3 (Student A):

You need to phone a restaurant to make a reservation for a business lunch your office is having next week. Your boss has asked that certain criteria be fulfilled: 1) If possible, you would like to have a separate banquet room for your group. There will be fifteen people. 2) You would like one large round table that will accommodate all 15 people. 3) You would like a set menu with a starter, main course and dessert, but you would like to have both a meat option and a fish option. This is for next Friday at 12:30pm. Your budget it $30 per person.

- Scenario 3 (Student B):

You work for Millennium Restaurant. You have a banquet room that seats 25 people. To reserve it, there is a fee of $100. You do not have any round tables; you only have rectangular tables. For a set menu you can offer: vegetable soup as a starter, beef and potatoes as a main dish and tiramisu for dessert. For a fish option, you can offer salmon and vegetables. The price is $28 per person plus the $100 rental fee for the banquet room.

- Scenario 4 (Student A):
You would like to reserve several hotel rooms for a conference at the Hotel California. You need four double rooms from May 2-May 5, preferably on the same floor. You would also like to reserve a meeting room for the morning of May 5 from 8:30 to 11:30am. You also need reservations at the hotel restaurant for 6 people on the evening of May 2 at 8pm. You don't want to pay more than $150 per night per room.

- Scenario 4 (Student B):
You work for Hotel California. You have four double rooms available between May 2 and May 5, but they are not on the same floor. Two are on the first floor and two are on the third floor. They cost $180 per night. You have a meeting room for 10 people. It is available on May 5 in the morning, but not in the afternoon. The hotel restaurant will be closed in May because of renovation work. Suggest a local restaurant and offer to make reservations.

9. Homework
Tell the students to revise the vocabulary for telephoning. You may want to have them prepare one of the role plays in writing, too, to check on their writing skills.

10. Vocabulary Bank

Telephone vocabulary:
- **To dial**: to push the numbers of the phone ring: sound a telephone makes
- **To answer**: to pick up the phone when it rings
- **To hang up**: to put down the phone at the end of your call
- **A busy line** (= an engaged line): when the person you want to speak to is already on the phone with someone else
- **To leave a message**: to give your name and number so the person will contact you
- **To call back**: to call again at a later time
- **To spell**: to give a word letter by letter A-L-Y-C-I-A
- **I didn't catch that**: I didn't understand what you said.
- **Could you repeat, please?**: Can you say it again, please?
- **Could you speak more slowly?** = Can you slow down?: Can you stop speaking so fast?

Chapter 4 – Communication (Lesson 2)

1. Introduction

In this section you will look at:
- How to e-mail in English

- What makes a good communicator

- How to give good oral presentations in English

In terms of grammar and vocabulary, you will review:
- Typical email vocabulary

- The modals to give advice for giving an effective presentation

2. Review of the Previous Lesson

Review the telephone vocabulary from the previous lesson.
If you decided to have them do one of the phone role plays in writing, have them exchange the role play with someone in order to correct them.

After they have corrected each other's role plays, you can collect them for final correction. This is a good way to see if they catch each other's mistakes (often they catch a few, but not all of them).

3. Group Discussion: E-mail Basics

If you feel they need some revision of the basics, you can go over the following questions with them:

a. How do you begin an e-mail? ("Dear Mr. Jones, Ms. Jones," if you know the person's name but you are not on a familiar basis with him; "Hi, John," if you are on familiar terms with the person. Remind them that e-mail is generally less formal than a letter.)

b. How do you end an e-mail? (Best regards, Kind regards, Regards; "Sincerely" or "Yours truly" are too formal.)

c. What do you say when you send a document with the e-mail? (Please find attached...)

d. Where do you write the topic of your e-mail? (in the subject bar)

e. What do we say if multiple recipients receive an e-mail, even if they are not directly addressed? (they are in copy)

f. What do you say when you put someone in copy but you don't want the recipient to know it? (in blind copy)

g. What does BTW stand for? (by the way)

h. What does ASAP stand for? (as soon as possible)

i. What does FYI stand for? (for your information)

4. Pair Work: E-mail Writing Practice

E-mails: In order to see how much the students know about e-mail writing, have them write an e-mail in pairs. Tell them to choose one of the telephone scenarios they did last time and work together to write a confirmation e-mail. Go over the e-mails as a group and see how they did.

5. Small Group Discussion: E-mails

a. Do you often write e-mails in English?
b. What kinds of difficulties can you have writing e-mails in English?
c. Do you take more care when writing e-mails in English?
d. Do you proofread your e-mails before you send them? In English? In your own language?
e. What are the advantages and disadvantages of working with e-mail?

6. Review of the Alphabet

Go over the letters that typically cause students difficulties (a, e, i, g, j, y, etc.). Remind them how to say the frequently used e-mail symbols (at [@], dot [.], underscore [_], dash [-]) and explain that in most cases people don't spell out the most common extensions; they just say them (.com, .net, .org, .co). Have the students work in pairs and dictate their e-mail addresses to each other. After they have practiced, give them a dictation as a class. I usually do two really tough ones and speak rather quickly just to remind them how important it is to review the letters. Tell them not to hesitate to ask their interlocutor to speak slowly or repeat. Some sample e-mail addresses are: eileen_gunderson@qktp.com, jeremiah.howe@astound.net, amelia-youngerston@jumpinjack.co.uk. Another extension of this activity is to pass out business cards to your students and have them dictate the name, address, e-mail address and phone number of the person with a partner.

7. Pair Work: E-mail Role Plays

Email exercises (you may want to give one or all of these for homework rather than having the students do the work in class):

1. You were interviewed for an internship a few weeks ago, but you haven't heard back from the company. You have tried to call several times, but your calls have not been returned. Write an e-mail to Mr. Johnson, the HR Manager, to inquire about your internship.

2. You heard about a new translation software that is more effective than Google Translate. You would like to know more about this software. Contact the company, Global Translate, to find out more details about the software including what it can do, the cost, etc. You are a little skeptical about it being foolproof, so ask some questions to reassure yourself.

3. You want to meet a friend for dinner and a movie tonight. Send her an e-mail to set it up.

4. Your boss has been out of the office a lot recently, and you have not been able to reach him by phone. You would like to set up a meeting with him, because you are having some problems with the project you are currently working on. Send him an email to set up a meeting.

8. Brainstorming: Good Communicators

What makes a good communicator ? Some possibilities are: use of voice, eloquence, charisma, eye contact, body language, natural hand gestures, etc.

Ask the students the best and worst presentations they have ever attended or seen. They can focus on someone famous like a politician, but they can also talk about a teacher or lecturer they have had (this usually gets them talking, especially if the teacher is not a very good public speaker). Get them talking about what made the speaker particularly good or bad.

9. Grammar Review: Modals

Take the opportunity to review must, mustn't, don't have to, should, shouldn't, etc. to make sure the students understand the meanings and uses. Have them work in pairs to come up with a list of suggestions for giving a good presentation using the modals.

Tell them to include the things you already mentioned above, but to also speak about the visual aids used during the presentation (Power Point, board, handouts, etc.). Sample list:

You should make eye contact with everyone in the audience, not just with one person. You don't have to have notes, but it might be a good idea so you don't get lost. You shouldn't read your notes. And so on.

Share the ideas as a group.

10. Interaction: Mini-Presentation

Tell them they are now going to put their suggestions to practice. They are going to have an opportunity to give a mini-presentation to the rest of the class based on one of their passions.

Here is the example I like to give them: "Hello, everyone! Thanks for coming today. Has anyone here ever been to San Francisco? Raise your hands. Well, I am going to speak to you about this city, because I love it. Yes, I was born there, but there is so much to see and do there that I'm sure you are going to want to buy a plane ticket at the end of my presentation. First I am going to speak about the tourist attractions that bring so many people to this city. After that, I am going to speak about the great eating opportunities and finally I am going to give you a few tips about the surrounding area and some things to visit in the San Francisco Bay Area."

After my intro, I ask the students to critique it. Have them focus on the importance of explaining exactly where you are going with your presentation. This will help the audience follow the talk, but it will also keep the speaker on track.

Give the class your own mini-presentation and have them critique it. After they have talked about it, give them 10-15 minutes to prepare a brief presentation about their passion. Tell them they will have 3-5 minutes to do the full presentation in front of the class, not just the intro.

After they have had a chance to prepare, choose three or four people at random to come up and do their presentation in front of the class. Have the rest of the class critique them. One of the things that should come up during the critique session is the fact that it was hard to feel confident in English with so little preparation time. One of the keys to a successful presentation is being well prepared.

11. Homework

Presentation Project
Divide the class into pairs and pass out the Persuasive Presentation paper. Explain to the class that they are going to be asked to give presentations in front of the class in pairs at a later date (you decide the timing for this and how many groups you want to pass each session; you can pass around a sign-up sheet for the students to sign up for specific dates). Be sure they understand what is expected. After they read the paper and ask some questions, if there is still some time left at the end of class, you can give the groups time to brainstorm possible subjects.

12. Persuasive Presentation

Working in pairs, you will give a 15-20-minute persuasive presentation on the subject of your choice. Your objective is to present both sides of an argument and then express your own standpoint. This will be followed by a question / debate session with the members of the audience. In your presentation, be sure to include SEVERAL questions to make people talk. If you can, try to avoid the subjects that have already been beaten to death (death penalty, abortion...). Choose an original topic!
Both presenters in the group need to have equal speaking time. Your grade will be based on the quality of your Power Point presentation (no spelling mistakes!), the strength of your arguments, correct grammar and vocabulary, good eye contact, eloquence, the quality of your debate, etc.

13. Vocabulary Bank

E-mail vocabulary:
- **Greeting**: a salutation, how you begin an e-mail
- **Subject bar**: where you write the main topic of your e-mail
- **Recipient**: the person who receives your e-mail
- **Carbon copy**: when you send a copy of your e-mail to another party or parties
- **Blind copy**: when you put someone in copy without the recipient being aware of it
- **BTW**: abbreviation for "by the way"
- **ASAP**: abbreviation for "as soon as possible"
- **FYI**: abbreviation for "for your information"

Chapter 5 – Management

1. Introduction

In this section you will look at:
- The role of managers and the management in a company

- How to work in a team and encourage team building

In terms of grammar and vocabulary, you will review:
- The past simple to talk about how managers used to work in the past

- Vocabulary related to management

- Vocabulary related to team building

2. Review of the Previous Lesson

Review the phone and e-mail vocabulary from the previous unit. If you are starting the persuasive presentations, you can do them before starting the new unit.

3. Brainstorming: Management

Write "Manager" on the board and have a brainstorming session with the students. Encourage them to say anything they think of related to managers and management.

4. Group Discussion: Managers

a. What is the role of a manager?

b. How should a manager relate to his/her team?

c. What are the qualities of a good manager? What makes a bad manager?

d. Describe the best/worst managers you have worked with. What was good/bad about the person?

e. What makes a successful manager?

f. Which management style(s) do you prefer? Why?

g. Do you think managers in different countries have different management styles?

h. How do you imagine they vary?

i. Do men or women make better managers? Why?

j. Would you like to be a manager? Why or why not?

k. Do you have what it takes to make a good manager? Why or why not?

5. Grammar Review: Past Simple

Review the rules for the past simple, and remind the class about the list of irregular verbs. In order to practice the past tense, ask them to think about how managers were different in the past. Work together as a class to come up with a list of things that were different before compared to today regarding management styles.

6. Pair Work: Qualities of a Good Manager

In pairs, have them come up with a list of suggestions for a good manager (A manager should be a good listener, etc.). Encourage them to come up with at least ten things and then compare the ideas with the rest of the class.

7. Group Discussion: Team Work

a. What are the positive points about working with a team?

b. What are the negative points about working with a team?

c. Discuss a good experience you have had working with a team. Why was it good?

d. Discuss a bad experience you have had working with a team. Why was it bad?

e. In your opinion, what is a "team player"? Are you a team player? Why or why not?

f. What are the different roles of the members of a team?

g. Is the manager always the team leader? What are the responsibilities of the team leader?

h. How should you deal with conflict within a team?

i. What are some potential problems you can have when working with a team?

j. How do you resolve these problems?

8. Role Plays: Managing and Being Managed

- Scenario 1 (Student A):
You are the manager of a team of ten people. Recently one of the members of the team has been making everyone else on the team miserable because of his negative attitude. He does excellent work, but he is not a team player. Meet with him to discuss this issue and to find a solution.

- Scenario 1 (Student B):
Your boss has asked to meet with you about some conflicts that have taken place within your team. You feel like you do all the work while the others take credit for it, and you are fed up. You think the rest of the team you work with does not have adequate skills for working on the projects you have to do. Explain your feelings to your boss.

- Scenario 2 (Student A):
Your mother has been in the hospital, which has been very difficult for you. Because of your family issues, you finished your section of a big project two days late. Rather than being understanding about this difficult period you are going through, your manager criticized you for being late. Speak to him about your impressions and feelings.

- Scenario 2 (Student B):
One of your employees turned in his section of an important project two days late. Because of the delay, the other people on the team were not able to complete their work. As a consequence, your company has to pay its client huge penalty sums. It is not the first time this employee has not managed to finish his part of a project on time.

- Scenario 3 (Student A):
You are the manager of a small team of three people. One of the people on the team has a defeatist attitude and spends all her time complaining. She thinks nothing will ever work and gripes about the tasks she is given to do. It has reached a point where she has become unbearable. Meet with her to discuss this problem.

- Scenario 3 (Student B):
Your boss has asked you for a meeting. You hope it is to give you a promotion, because you have been in the same position and pay bracket for three years now.

9. Homework

Tell the students to revise the management vocabulary. For a writing assignment, you can have them write a paragraph entitled "The Ideal Boss" to focus on the qualities you covered during the lesson.

10. Vocabulary Bank

Management vocabulary:
- **To delegate**: to have another person do a task under your supervision
- **Empowerment**: a feeling of enablement or ability
- **Team**: a number of people working together for a common goal
- **Synergy**: cooperative interaction among people or groups
- **Subordinate**: an employee of a lower rank
- **Leader**: a person who manages or inspires others
- **Hierarchical structure**: organization where the top managers carry the most responsibility and the lower levels follow those managers' dictates
- **Drive**: energy or force
- **Efficient**: capable, competent
- **Matrix management**: cross-functional management structure which is based on transversal management rather than hierarchical management
- **Top management**: highest managers in a company
- **Middle management**: managers below the top managers

Chapter 6 - Project Management

1. Introduction

In this section you will look at:
- How to deal with project management

- Methods for creating a reverse planning

In terms of grammar and vocabulary, you will review:
- The conditionals

- Vocabulary related to project management

2. Review of the Previous Lesson

Review the management vocabulary from the previous unit. Collect "The Ideal Boss" paragraphs they wrote to correct them. Another option would be to have them exchange their paragraphs with another student and correct each other's documents before turning them in.

3. Pair Work: Planning a Forum

Tell the students the subject for the day is project management.

Have them work in pairs to discuss the following situation: You and your team have been asked to plan a week-long business forum at your university.

If your students are business people, you can adapt the scenario to a week-long forum in their company with suppliers, counterparts, competitors, etc.

The objective of the forum is to invite business people from various fields and sectors to come to the school to meet with students to talk about the business world.

There will be various key-note speakers, conferences with a variety of subjects and meals to organize, as well as the invitations and the physical location of the event.

Work with a partner to brainstorm the tasks that will need to be completed in order to have a successful event.

After they have spoken, have them share their thoughts with the class. Questions related to the discussion:

a. What would be the biggest challenge about organizing such an event?

b. What are the things you must take into consideration? (budget, timing, number of people, etc.)

c. What problems do you think you might encounter during the organization of the forum?

d. Would you enjoy doing something like this? Why or why not?

4. Small Group Discussion: Projects

a. Have you ever worked on a group project?

b. If so, what did you like/dislike about it?

c. How did you organize yourselves?

d. Who was the leader of the group? How was this person selected? What was his/her role?

e. What was the easiest part about working with a group? The most difficult?

f. What are the pros and cons of working with a team and working alone?
Compare the answers with the rest of the class.

5. Brainstorming: Working with a Reverse Planning

Write "reverse planning" on the board and ask the class to define it.

Ask them why this method is useful.

Talk about the types of projects a reverse planning might be used for (anything really, but especially projects with multiple tasks and distant deadlines).

Have them explain how this method might be organized (the importance of starting from the final date and working backwards to map out all the tasks for a given project).

Tell the students they are going to map out the reverse planning for the business forum they spoke about above.

Tell them they have three months to plan the event.

Have them make a time line and imagine what needs to be done when, working backward from the day of the event (caterer, speakers, meeting room or conference center, business contacts, invitations, etc.).

They should use the information they brainstormed in activity 2 as a base for their reverse planning. Have them compare their map with another group and then with the rest of the class.

6. Listening: Completing a Project on Time

Project Management (audio files found on the ASAP Coaching video site; see link at the back of the book in the bonus section to have access).

Transcript: Joshua Miller is the leader of a seven-person team that is creating a geo-location application for Smart phones. They have a tight deadline, and Joshua is trying to establish the reverse planning for the completion of the project.

- All right, Mark. Are we ready to go ahead with the test phase?
- Unfortunately, there have been a few glitches during the last steps of the development phase. We are not quite ready to begin testing.
- How much time do you think you need?
- We should be able to wrap things up in the next five days.
- Make it two.
- I'll try, but I can't make any promises.
- We are supposed to go live in a month, and we need a month for the test phase. What is the problem?
- Um, well, the app is not exactly compatible with Apple devices.
- What!? That's not a glitch; that's a disaster!
- It sounds worse than it is. We just need to tinker a bit. It shouldn't take long to find a solution.
- Are you sure about that? Our client expects this to be ready to market in 30 days. For each day beyond that, we have to pay exorbitant penalties.
- I know the stakes, and we are doing everything humanly possible to finish on time.
- You'd better. Let's meet tomorrow so you can tell me what progress you've made.
- Let's meet in two days. If I spend all my time meeting with you, I'm not working on the app!

7. Group Discussion: Project Management Problems

a. Are projects often late?

b. What kind of consequences can a company face if they don't finish a project on time?

c. Have you ever had to deal with a tough deadline for a project? How did you deal with it?

8. Grammar Review: Conditionals

Review the 1st, 2nd and 3rd conditional on the board. (If it rains, I will go to the cinema. If I won the lottery, I would buy a new house. If I hadn't started my new job, I would have traveled around the world.) Go around and ask the students some sample questions to make sure they understand the three structures.

9.

10. Discussion Questions (with 2nd conditional)

a. If you had to work on a group project, would you rather be the project leader or just a member of the team?

b. If you had a limited amount of time to complete a project, what would your strategy be?

c. If you had a choice between working alone and working with a team, which would you choose?

d. If you were project manager, what management skills would you use with your team?

e. If you had a conflict on your team, how would you deal with it?

11. Homework

Tell the students to revise the project management vocabulary for the next lesson.

12. Vocabulary Bank

Project Management
- **Reverse planning**: planning that starts with the end of the project and looks at all the milestones of events that need to be completed between now and then
- **Suppliers**: provide a product or service for a company (For example, a clothing store may have suppliers in a developing country. Those suppliers manufacture and sell them the clothes they will in turn sell in their shops.)
- **Counterpart**: a person who does the same job as you in another company
- **Competitor**: a company that does the same activity as your company and could potentially attract your customers
- **Caterer**: company that provides food and service for individuals or other companies (We had a caterer prepare the buffet for our office Christmas party.)
- **Glitch**: a problem
- **To wrap something up**: to finish something
- **To go live**: to go on line officially
- **To tinker**: to make adjustments
- **Stakes**: a right or legal share of something; a financial involvement with something

Chapter 7 – Marketing

1. Introduction

In this section you will look at:
- The four Ps

- Advertising

In terms of grammar and vocabulary, you will review:
- Structure of present perfect

- Present perfect and superlative

- Vocabulary related to marketing and advertising

2. Review of the Previous Lesson

Review the Project Management vocabulary from the previous lesson. You may want to combine the vocabulary from previous units, as well, to make sure they are retaining all the new words.

3. Brainstorming: The 4 Ps

Write "the 4 Ps" on the board and ask the students if they know what that means. Help elicit the four words: product, price, place, promotion. Give them the example of a product. You can use anything. Ask them where they would find the chosen product, how much it would cost and how they would inform people about the product. For example: product: coffee; price: around $4.00 depending on the brand; place: supermarket, in the breakfast aisle; promotion: point-of-sale display). This can lead to a discussion about different ways to promote a product (point-of-sale display, price reduction, free samples, advertising, social networks, word-of-mouth, publicity, coupons, etc.). You can also talk about how the concept of promotion has changed because of technology (social networks, Internet advertising, etc.).

4. Group Discussion: Marketing

a. What is the objective of marketing?

b. What do you think are the most effective marketing techniques?

c. Do you ever make impulsive purchases that are influenced by marketing strategies?

d. What do you think about using social media to market products?

e. What is your opinion about advertising?

f. What is the best/worst ad that you can remember?

g. What makes a good ad?

h. Do you think ads manipulate us?

i. What influence do you think ads have on children?

5. Grammar Review: Present Perfect

Write "to have + past participle" on the board. Ask the following questions related to advertising and marketing:

a. Have you ever bought a product after seeing an ad?

b. Have you ever used a social network to publicize an event?

c. Have you ever bought something you didn't need because of a promotion?

Review the superlatives from Lesson 3 and then practice the superlatives with the present perfect:
a. What is the funniest commercial you have ever seen?

b. What is the worst commercial you have ever seen?

c. What is the strangest promotion you have ever seen?

d. What is the most shocking ad you have ever seen?

e. What is the most useless product you have ever bought?

f. What is the best deal you have ever had thanks to a promotion?

6. Listening: Advertising Campaign

Marketing (audio files found on the ASAP Coaching video site; see link at the back of the book in the bonus section to have access).

Transcript: Jackie Larsen is the advertising manager of Playco, a toy store chain. She and her team are brainstorming about an ad campaign for Christmas.

- We need something new this year. Aside from a few small changes, we have used the same lay-out in the catalogue for the past three years.
- But it works. Our Christmas sales have increased each year since we published the catalogue.
- True, but I think we can do even better this year.
- How?
- Well, this lay-out is quite classical. Why don't we use some brighter colors and a more extravagant font, something that would appeal to kids.
- It needs to appeal to the parents, too. They are the ones with the money!
- Of course, but if the kids like it, they will beg their parents to buy it.
- I am not opposed to trying something new. Why don't you put something together and bring it to our next meeting?
- Actually, I already started. I only worked on a few pages, but I think the result is pretty good.
- Hmmm. We have never done anything like this before. I'm not sure our customers are ready for such flashy colors.
- I don't agree. I think it will attract their attention, and the colors match our image.
- Let me think about it. Let's show this to the rest of the team and get their opinion.

7. Small Group Discussion: Advertising

a. What do you think of companies that target children in their advertising?

b. Should an ad target the kids or the parents?

c. Do you think catalogues are still an effective form of advertising?

8. Small Group Work: Create a Product

Break the students into groups of 3. Tell them they are going to create a new innovative food product. You can choose a particular kind of cuisine or regional dishes if that will help them choose a product. It can be something you can find in the supermarket or a restaurant. After they brainstorm what product they would like to create, they should decide:
a. Their target audience—who will buy the product?

b. The price

c. The packaging

d. The logo

e. How they plan to launch the product on the market

f. Why their product is innovative

g. Who their competitors will be

h. Their advertising campaign (they should include a TV commercial for the product which they will perform in front of the class)

i. In which foreign countries will they try and launch this product? How will their marketing strategies differ according to the country?

Give the groups time to come up with their product and campaign and then have them do the presentations in front of the class.

9. Homework

Tell the students to study the vocabulary related to marketing and advertising for the next lesson. If some groups did not have time to present their product, tell them they will do so during the next lesson.

10. Vocabulary Bank

Marketing vocabulary:
- **Product**: what is being sold
- **Price**: how much the product costs
- **Place**: where the product is found in the store
- **Promotion**: a way to publicize or advertise a product
- **Brand**: trademark
- **Point-of-sale display**: special place where products are displayed, usually near the cash register, as part of a promotion
- **Free sample**: a small portion of a product given for free in order to promote it to the public
- **Social network**: an on-line network like Facebook
- **Word of mouth**: when one person tells another and so on
- **Packaging**: what a product is wrapped in
- **To launch a product**: to put a product on the market for the first time
- **Consumer**: person who buys products
- **Distributors**: companies which sell their products to stores for mass consumption
- **End-user**: consumer
- **Market research**: studying the buying habits of customers

Advertising vocabulary:
- **Advertisement** (=advert, ad): paid announcement to sell a product or service
- **Commercial**: ad on television or the radio
- **Advertising agency**: company that creates ads
- **Billboard**: large board used for advertising
- **Campaign**: a series of advertising activities to sell a product
- **Direct mail**: sending ads directly to customers via post
- **Mass media**: all forms of media including radio, TV, newspaper, etc.

Chapter 8 – Sales

1. Introduction

In this section you will look at:
- Sales strategies

- Negotiations

- E-commerce

In terms of grammar and vocabulary, you will review:
- Reported speech

- Vocabulary related to sales

2. Review of the Previous Lesson

Review the Marketing and Advertising vocabulary from the previous lesson. If any of the groups have not presented their product to the class, you can begin the lesson with that.

3. Brainstorming: Sales Strategy

Ask the class to define "sales strategy". What things does a salesperson need to consider when trying to make a sale? (establishing a rapport with the client, what the salesperson has to offer, how much he wants for it, how much his client wants what he is selling, how much negotiating room he has, etc.)

Write "negotiation" on the board. Ask the students what kinds of things they negotiate in their daily lives (for example: I'll cook dinner if you do the dishes.)

4. Group Discussion (in pairs or as a class): Negotiating

a. Do you like negotiating? Why or why not?

b. Do you consider yourself to be a good negotiator? Why or why not?

c. Do you like bargaining prices at markets (very typical in developing countries)?

d. What are the qualities of a good negotiator?

e. What should you consider before you begin a negotiation? (limits, compromise, price, etc.)

f. How important is compromise in the negotiation process?

g. Can stubborn people be good negotiators?

h. What is the best / worst negotiating experience you have ever had?

i. Would you like to have a job where you have to negotiate on a regular basis? Why or why not?

5. Role Plays: Negotiation

Break the class into pairs and have them do the following role plays. You may want to choose a few groups to perform their negotiation in front of the class after they have taken some time to prepare.

- Scenario 1 (Student A)
You work in the purchasing department for a clothing retail shop in the US. You need 1,000 t-shirts (250 black, 250 white, 250 gray, 100 red, 100 navy blue and 50 light blue). You would like to pay $3.00 per t-shirt. You need them delivered 30 days after confirmation of the order.

- Scenario 1 (Student B)
You are a supplier. You can manufacture 1,000 t-shirts at $4.00 a shirt. For orders of more than 1,000 t-shirts, the price goes down to $3.00 per article. All colors are available except light blue. Normal delivery time is 45 days.

- Scenario 2 (Student A)
You work for B to B Voyages, a travel agency that arranges business trips for companies. Your clients are big firms with a large volume of trips, and the great majority of your passengers are executives. You have a new exclusive package you are selling which includes business class seats for long haul flights and premium rooms in top hotels worldwide. You are trying to convince a long-standing client to upgrade their top management and use the exclusive package. The average price they pay for the existing travel packages is $1,000 per trip for airfare and hotel. The exclusive package would take that price up to $2,000, but the new loyalty programme linked to the

exclusive packages could save the company $10,000 a year if they can guarantee 100 trips with the new package.

- Scenario 2 (Student B)
You work for Fresh Life, a food industry company that has subsidiaries all over the world. Your staff takes an average of 250 trips per year. All these trips, including hotel and airfare, are booked through B to B Voyages. This represents a huge budget, and you would like to reduce the amount of money spent each year on travel. However, the top executives of the company are more and more demanding about the quality of travel. Try to find a solution with B to B Voyages.

- Scenario 3 (Student A)
You are a corporate banker. You are meeting with a prospective client to see what his financial needs are. It is a metal works company, and such companies have been doing poorly in the past few years. Your bank is pushing bank loans, so see what interests him. Presently the interest rate is 3.5%.

- Scenario 3 (Student B)
You are CFO of a metal works company. You aren't happy with the services offered by your current bank, so you are meeting with a banker from another bank to see what he has to offer. In order for your company to develop, you need a big bank loan of $1.5 million. You would like a 3% rate for such a loan.

6. Listening: Convincing a Client

Sales (audio files found on the ASAP Coaching video site; see link at the back of the book in the bonus section to have access).

Transcript: Johan Evans works for Prima Organics, a company that sells ready-made organic meals to organic supermarkets. He's meeting with Gretchen Slackston, purchasing manager of Green Grocers Plus, an organic grocery store chain.

- We have a new line of products we are launching next month. It's our 'international line'.
- Okay, sounds interesting. What exactly is it?
- They are microwave meals from all over the world. There is 'Tofu Parmesan' from Italy, 'Veggie Curry Delight' from India, 'Tofu Pad Thai' from Thailand and 'Pho Pot' from Vietnam.
- Sounds interesting. What kind of pricing are we talking about?
- We can sell them to you at $5.00 a meal. I know that sounds like a lot, but we are convinced customers are ready to pay $8.00 a meal in the store. That would leave you a great margin.
- You're right. It would leave us a great margin if I thought our customers would pay that much. $8.00 is huge.
- Something you need to take into consideration is the portion size. These meals actually represent two portion sizes. You can sell them as a 'double sized' meal.
- Even if that is true, I'm not sure we can sell them at that price. What's your lowest common denominator?
- I'm afraid $5.00 *is* our lowest price.
- Well, if that is true, the only thing I can agree with is a test. We take a limited number of meals and see what kind of response we have.
- Sure. If you would agree to purchase 100 meals to see how your customers respond, we could take stock after a week.

- I was thinking more along the lines of 50 meals.
- All right, we can do 50. But I am convinced that you will be begging me for more.
- We'll see.

7. Group Discussion: E-commerce

a. Do you shop on line? If so, what do you buy?

b. Is there anything that you would refuse to buy on line?

c. How has e-commerce changed the way we do business?

d. Do you prefer buying something on line or from a bricks and mortar shop?

e. What effect do you think e-commerce will have on bricks and mortar shops in the future?

f. Do you think bricks and mortar shops will disappear? Why or why not?

8. Homework

Tell the students to study the vocabulary related to sales for the next lesson.

9. Vocabulary Bank

Sales vocabulary:
- **Negotiation**: mutual discussion to come to a final satisfactory agreement for both parties
- **To bargain**: to discuss the final price, often in an outdoor market
- **Compromise**: agreement made by both sides making concessions
- **Stubborn**: hard-headed
- **After sales service**: department responsible for customer care after the purchase of a product
- **Buyer**: person who buys, usually for a company (= purchaser)
- **Client / Customer**: client is usually for a law firm, bank or B to B client; customer is generally used for the consumers who buy the products directly in the shop
- **Cold call**: calling prospects you don't know to try to make a sale
- **Deal**: business transaction
- **Discount**: reduced price
- **Guarantee**: a promise of quailty
- **Product / Service**: a product is a good; a service is usually not something tangible
- **Prospect**: a potential client or customer
- **Retail**: sale of goods to end-users, usually in small quantities
- **Wholesale**: sales of goods to retailers, usually in large quantities

Chapter 9 - Human Resources (Lesson 1)

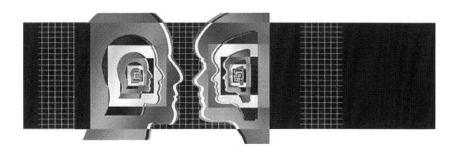

1. Introduction

In this section you will look at:
- Recruitment and hiring

- CVs and cover letters

- Job interviews

In terms of grammar and vocabulary, you will review:
- Time clauses

- Vocabulary related to recruitment and hiring

2. Review of the Previous Lesson

Review the sales vocabulary from the previous lesson.

3. Group Discussion: Looking for a Job

Start the discussion by asking what people should do if they are interested in looking for a job. (update their CV, write a cover letter, look at job announcements on the Internet, post their CV on a suitable web-site, etc.).

Discuss what information should be included on a CV (no photo, DOB, age, marital status, nationality). Ask the students what order they think things should appear (reverse chronological order from the most recent to the oldest: Education, Work experience, Skills, Extracurricular Activities). Be sure to explain that they should not use complete sentences. Rather than saying "I analyzed data", they should just say "analyzed data". See if they have any questions about specific vocabulary and then tell them they will need to bring their CV in English to the next lesson. Remind them that their CV should not exceed one page.

Begin a discussion about cover letters.
a. What information should be included in a cover letter? (your address, company address, salutation, signature...).

b. What is the best salutation to use? (If you know the person's name, Dear Mr. Jones, Dear Ms. Smith. If you don't know the person's name: Dear Sir or Madam or To Whom It May Concern)

c. What should you include in the main body of the letter? (first paragraph: why you are writing and the position you are applying for; second paragraph: why you suit the job being offered; third paragraph: thank them for their consideration and let them know you will contact them to follow-up)

d. How should you end a cover letter? (Sincerely, Respectfully yours...)

e. How long should a cover letter be? (no more than one page)

f. What are some common mistakes people make when writing cover letters? (spelling or grammar mistakes, copying their CV word for word, forgetting to put contact information...)

You will need to decide if you want your students to do both the CV and the cover letter for the following lesson. If that seems like too much, you can have them write the cover letter for the following lesson. The best things to do is have them choose a job announcement (for a job or an internship depending on their level and age) that they are actually interested in and to write a cover letter for that job.

4. Grammar Review: Time Clauses

Remind the students about the first conditional (If it rains, I will go shopping: first part of the sentence in the present, second part in the future). Tell them this is the same case for other subordinate clauses, as well (as soon as, after, before, until, when, while). Explain that "while" is often used with the present continuous because it represents an idea of something that is going on at the moment.

5. Pair Work: Practice Questions Related to Job Interviews

a. What will you do when you graduate?

b. What will you do as soon as you finish this lesson?

c. What will you do before you start your first job?

d. What will you do after you have your first job interview?

e. What will you do while your teacher is explaining about job interviews?

6. Group Discussion: Job Interviews

a. Do you like job interviews? Why or why not?

b. What's the best / worst interview you have ever had?

c. What are the questions you enjoyed answering?

d. What are the most difficult questions you have had?

7. Pair Work: Mock Job Interviews

Divide the class into pairs and have them brainstorm a list of 10 typical interview questions. Tell them to each write their list of questions down, as they will be split into different groups for the interview role plays. After they have finished their lists, break the group into different pairs and have them interview each other. After they have each had an opportunity to be both interviewer and interviewee, come back together as a class to discuss the experience.

Questions regarding interview:
a. What were the difficult questions?

b. What were the easy questions?

c. Were there any questions you were not able to answer?

d. What did you learn from this role play? (I assume they will comment on the importance of being prepared!)

8. (Small) Group Discussion: Tough Questions

At this point, I often add a list of my own tough questions. If the group is small enough you can ask them each a question that they have to answer in front of the class. It puts them on the spot, but it's a good reminder of the importance of preparing for an interview. If you have a big group, you can choose some students at random and ask them a question to answer in front of the class. They may have done some of the questions during their role play, but that doesn't matter. Practice makes perfect!

a. Tell me the three adjectives that best describe you.

b. What are your strengths and weaknesses?

c. Tell me about something you've done recently that you are proud of.

d. What is the biggest challenge you have had to deal with during your studies (or career)? How did you deal with it?

e. Tell me about a problem you had recently. How did you solve it?

f. If you could erase one day from your existence, which day would you erase and why? (If this is too personal, tell them they don't have to share.)

g. Are you a team player or a lone ranger?

h. Where do you see yourself in 5 years? 10 years?

i. Rate the last manager you worked with. Why was he a good / bad manger?

j. What are your expectations regarding salary?

k. Tell me about one of your passions. How has this passion shaped who you are?

l. Why should I give you this job?

9. Listening 1: The Bad Interview

Job Interview 1 (audio files found on the ASAP Coaching video site; see link at the back of the book in the bonus section to have access).

Transcript: Doreen Hansen is interviewing Oliver Jones for a quality assistant position.

- Tell me about yourself, Oliver.
- Well, I am in my last year of school. My ultimate goal is to land a job as quality manager. I'm pretty sure it won't take me long to get there.
- Hmmm. Sounds ambitious. What experience do you have in the field?
- I did a six-month internship at Cracker 'N More in the quality department. I was responsible for a total revamping of the quality process.
- Impressive. What exactly did that entail?
- Um, well, you know. Improving the current process.
- Can you give me a little more information?
- Sure. I um, well, I looked at the former process and made comments about it. Then I wrote a new one.
- Uh huh. So, Oliver, what are your strengths and weaknesses?
- Well, I'm hard-working and motivated. I put everything I have into finishing a job. I am also energetic and dynamic.
- Okay. What about your weaknesses?
- Um, well I guess the biggest would be that I am a perfectionist. I won't stop working on something until it is perfect.
- I see. And what salary would you expect?
- Well, I figure the salary of a quality manager is fair. I mean, I'll be doing essentially the same job, right?
- Hmm. So, why should we choose you for the job over the other applicants we have?

- Well, I should think that's obvious. Because I'm the best!

10. Listening 2: The Good Interview

Job Interview 2 (audio files found on the ASAP Coaching video site; see link at the back of the book in the bonus section to have access).

Transcript:
Doreen Hansen is interviewing Jake Keller for a quality assistant position.

- Tell me about yourself, Jake.
- I am from New York, and I am currently in my last year of school. I play basketball and soccer, and I am involved in the junior enterprise club at my school.
- Why do you think you are a good applicant for this job?
- I have focused on quality during my studies, and last year I did an internship at Yoplait for 6 months. It was a great experience because I had a chance to really see how a quality department works.
- What exactly did you do there?
- Whatever they needed me to! Sometimes they needed me in the lab to analyze products. Sometimes I accompanied the quality manager to the factory to evaluate the production process. I tried to learn as much as I could during my time there and to help wherever they needed me.
- What was the most interesting part of your experience?
- Um, I think that would be seeing the process from beginning to end. When you work in quality, you need to know all the aspects of the process, and I really had a chance to observe that.
- What was the most difficult part of your experience?
- I suppose knowing that I would be leaving, so I would never see the continuity of the process. I had to leave a number of projects to other colleagues when my internship ended. It was disappointing not being able to see them through.

- What are your qualities and faults?
- I'm a good listener, which I think is important not only at the work place, but in my life in general. As for my faults, I suppose one of the worst would be linked to my quality. Sometimes I spend too much time listening, so I am not as reactive as I could be. I am working on that, because I know it's important to react quickly, especially at work.
- Why should we choose you for this job?
- Because I will give you everything I have to do the best job possible.

11. Group Discussion: Interview Debriefing

a. Which applicant would you take? Why?

b. What did Oliver and Jake do right / wrong?

c. What should they have done differently to have a better interview?

12. Homework

Tell the students to study the vocabulary related to recruiting and job interviews for the next lesson.
If you have decided that you want to do their CV and/or coverletter, have them prepare the documents for next time.

13. Vocabulary Bank

Recruitment and hiring vocabulary:
- **Applicant**: person applying for a job; candidate
- **To apply for a job**: to present yourself for a job
- **To appoint a person**: to offer a job to someone
- **To be dismissed**: to lose your job
- **To be laid off**: to lose your job, usually because of economic problems in the company
- **To be on probation**: to be on trial at the beginning of a new job
- **Overtime pay**: money earned for working extra hours
- **Pay slip**: document a salaried employee receives at the end of the month with his salary and contributions indicated on it
- **To resign / to give notice**: to quit your job
- **To retire**: to stop working at the end of your career
- **Salaried employees**: person who works for a company for a monthly salary
- **Sick leave**: period of time an employee does not work due to illness
- **Trade union**: an organization of workers who work together to protect their jobs

Chapter 10 - Human Resources (Lesson 2)

1. Introduction

In this section you will look at:
- Training

- Performance appraisal

In terms of grammar and vocabulary, you will review:
- Relative clauses

- Vocabulary related to training and staff evaluations

2. Review of the Previous Lesson

Review the HR vocabulary from the previous lesson. It may be a good time to give them a pop quiz to keep them on their toes.

Collect their CVs and cover letters to correct them. Another option would be to have them exchange the documents with another student to correct and critique them.

3. Brainstorming: Training

Write "training" on the board. Tell the students you are going to talk about human resources and training. Ask them what kind of training sessions companies can offer their staff (management training, language classes, stress management, time management, technical training based on the employees' field, etc.). Ask them if they think such training is important. Why or why not? What is the target of a company providing its staff with training courses? If the students could take a training course, what would they be interested in taking?

4. Small Group Discussion: Annual Training Program
Planning an annual training program.

Have the students work in small groups. Tell them they work in the training section of an HR Department in a mid-size company (100 employees), and they have to map out the year's training program.
First have them brainstorm how they would organize such an undertaking and what things they would need to take into consideration.
Give them freedom to do this without giving them any hints initially.

After they have come up with a game plan, have each group compare ideas with the rest of the class. (Ideally, they will speak about the importance of having a budget.

They should also come up with a way to ascertain the various needs of the staff: on-line or paper questionnaires, requests from the managers of each department for specific training courses for their staff, etc.

They should present how the intend to obtain and collect the information, and then how they would select the appropriate courses.)

5. Group Discussion: Training Programs

a. How would you deal with it if a staff member requested one training course and his manager wanted him to do something completely different?

b. What are your expectations of a training course? (clear objectives, precise timing, professional trainers, pertinent material, useful feedback at the end of the course for the staff member, his manager and the HR Department...)

c. How can you be sure the employee achieved his objectives? (ask for a progress report from the training center, for example)

d. How do you think the system would differ in a big company? (In really big companies, they usually have a training catalogue on the company intranet, which includes all the training sessions available during the year. It would be too difficult to collect individual requests from every person. They tend to have employees choose training sessions from the catalogue, and then validate the choices with the staff member's direct manager.)

6. Role Plays: Training

- Scenario 1 (Student A)
You are interested in taking English training courses for your job. You deal with suppliers in China and Bangladesh on almost a daily basis, and you what some phone and email practice. You feel that you have some issues with comprehension and a lack of vocabulary. Talk to your manager about your needs.

- Scenario 1 (Student B)
One of your purchasing managers would like to take English lessons. He already has an excellent level or English—all he needs is a little self-confidence. You don't think he needs lessons, and at any rate, there is no budget for him to do so. Be as diplomatic as possible when explaining this.

- Scenario 2 (Student A)
You have spoken to your manager about taking stress management training courses. He feels that you don't need these courses. He would like you to take time management courses instead. You don't feel that this will be sufficient; you have been more and more stressed lately. You have decided to approach the HR Manager directly to discuss your concerns.

- Scenario 2 (Student B)
You are HR Manager. A staff member has approached you because she is interested in taking a stress management training course. Her manager does not agree with her choice. Speak to her about the possibilities.

7. Group Discussion: Yearly Performance Appraisal

Tell the class that another aspect of HR is the yearly performance appraisal. Ask the class to define this. (annual assessment of employees' work performance).

Discussion questions:
a. Why do you think yearly performance appraisals are important?

b. How do you think the process usually works? (In most cases, both the employee and the manager fill out a form to evaluate the achievement (or non achievement) of the year's objectives. They look at these forms together during the face to face interview to see if they are on the same page.)

c. What are common subjects during a yearly performance appraisal? (objectives, attitude and behavior, respect of company values, training courses for the coming year and perhaps bonus and pay rise—though the financial aspect is often raised at a later date after all the performance appraisals have been completed)

d. What if there is a conflict between the employee and the manager during the appraisal, for example if the employee does not agree with the manager's assessment? (this would be noted in the documents and signed by both parties, but they do not have to reach a compromise; their difference of opinion must be in writing for any future issues.)

8. Listening: Yearly Performance Appraisal

Yearly Performance Appraisal (audio files found on the ASAP Coaching video site; see link at the back of the book in the bonus section to have access).

Transcript:
Greg Buis is conducting a yearly performance appraisal with Anne Kelley, a member of his team.

- How are you feeling about the work you did last year?
- Pretty good. I met three of the four objectives we established at the beginning of the year well ahead of schedule, and the only reason I didn't complete the fourth one is because the management tabled the project due to budget constraints.
- Absolutely. There is nothing you could have done about it. Though, between you and me, the project might be back on the table next year.
- Really? That's great. I thought they'd decided it was more money than they wanted to spend.
- Yes, well, we had a better quarter than expected, so they are reconsidering. Which leads me to our next subject. Let's talk about your objectives for next year.
- I assume the Tech Team launch will be one of those objectives—if the management decides to go through with it.
- Yes. In addition, I have an ambitious plan for launching two new applications before the end of the first semester.
- OK, I'll bite. What are they?
- Before I get into that, I have an important question. How would you feel about leading your own team?
- I would love it. How many people?
- Three. I think you'll need that many to get these two projects live on time. Of course, your salary will adapt to your new role. I can't give you an exact figure just yet, but I'm sure we can make it worth your while.

- Sounds good. Now tell me about these applications.

Discussion questions:
a. Do you think bonuses and pay rises are a good way to encourage employees to work harder?

b. Would you prefer a big one-time bonus or a pay rise? Why?

c. Which is more important, praise or a raise? Why?

9. Grammar Review: Relative Clauses

Write the following sentences on the board:

- John works for a company which makes a lot of money.

- John works for a company that makes a lot of money.

- John is an employee who makes a lot of money. = John is an employee that makes a lot of money.

- Remind the students that while they can use "that" in either case, they need to use "which" for an object and "who" for a person.

10. Homework

Tell the students to study the vocabulary related to training and yearly performance appraisals for the next lesson.

11. Vocabulary Bank

Training vocabulary:
- **Trainer**: a person who teaches something
- **Trainee**: a person who learns something
- **Training course**: a class targeted at learning a specific skill
- **Feedback**: response to a task of activity
- **Career development**: moving forward in your job
- **Coaching**: assistance in a specific field
- **Competency assessment**: evaluation of skills
- **Continuous learning**: learning after the typical school training
- **Skills**: competences

Yearly performance appraisal vocabulary:
- **Appraisal**: evaluation
- **Objectives**: targets or goals set at the beginning of the year
- **Absenteeism**: when an employee does not come to work
- **Rating**: score given during a yearly performance appraisal
- **Best practices**: best method possible for doing a given task
- **Overqualified**: having too many qualifications
- **Underqualified**: not having enough qualifications
- **Track record**: past record of failures / accomplishments

Chapter 11 - Finance and Banking

1. Introduction

In this section you will look at:
- The financial sector

- Bank products and services

In terms of grammar and vocabulary, you will review:
- Quantifiers (much, many, few, little)

- Vocabulary related to finance and banking

2. Review of the Previous Lesson

Go over the training and yearly performance appraisal vocabulary from the previous lesson to make sure all the new words are clear.

3. Brainstorming: Finance

Write "finance" on the board, and have a brainstorming session to elicit as much vocabulary as possible. You may need to ask questions or provide them with some words (examples: bank, stocks, shares, the stock market, traders, Wall Street, loans, mortgages, financial advisor, interest rates, etc.)

4. Group Discussion: Banking

You can have them work in small groups or do them as a class.
a. How difficult is it to get a bank loan in your country?

b. How difficult is it to get a mortgage? What is the typical duration of a mortgage?

c. What is an interest rate? Are the interest rates low or high at present?

d. Do people typically refinance their mortgages in your country? Do you think this is a good thing or a bad thing?

e. If you had to choose what to do with your extra money, would you:
  i. open a savings account?
  ii. invest in the stock market?
  iii. invest in a real estate project?
  iiii. hide it under your mattress?

f. What is the attitude about money in your country? Is it a taboo subject?

g. Does the banking sector have a good reputation in your country?

5. Review of Numbers

Write some numbers on the board to make sure the students know how to say them. Highlight the difference between 13 and 30, 14 and 40, etc. Review the hundreds, thousands and millions. Once you are sure the students know the numbers, do a dictation. Read the following numbers and have the students write down what they hear in number form. Speak at a normal speed and repeat as needed. Some sample figures might be: 550,113; 11,009,112; 30, 014.

6. Listening: Making an Investment

Finance (audio files found on the ASAP Coaching video site; see link at the back of the book in the bonus section to have access).

Transcript: Ryan Jacobs is meeting with Michelle Hayes, a financial advisor, to talk about investing a sum of money he inherited from his grandmother.

- You said you are wary about investing in the stock market.
- It's such a mess these days. I would hate to lose everything my grandmother left me if the market crashed.
- Not all stock investments are risky. What about some long-term 'rocking chair' investments?
- 'Rocking chair'?
- It's a term I like to use for 'safe' stocks. There is not a huge return, so they are really not interesting in the short-term. However, they become interesting if you don't touch them over a long period of time. They are stocks that tend to have gradual increases over the years.
- I don't know. What other options do I have?
- You could always put it in an IRA.
- What would that entail?
- The money would be tied up for a certain period of time, so you would need to make sure you don't need any cash in the short term.
- What about real estate investments? I have heard that buying rental properties has a good return on investment.
- Absolutely. Of course it depends on where you buy, but you have enough money to invest in real estate, no problem. Do you have anything specific in mind?
- Not yet. I will have a look at the housing market and get back to you.

7. Role Plays: At the Bank

- Scenario 1 (Student A)
You are a banker. A customer would like to open a checking account. Your bank offers free checkbooks, renewable at any time during the year, but your banks cards carry a $50 annual fee. Try to convince him to open a savings account, as well. Current interest rates are 1.25%.

- Scenario 1 (Student B)
You would like to open a current account. You need a checkbook and a bank card. You don't want to have to pay for either. You might be interested in opening a savings account if they can guarantee an interest rate higher than 1.5%.

- Scenario 2 (Student A)
You would like a loan to buy a new car. You can put $10,000 down, so you need a $20,000 loan for the rest. You want a 10-year loan with a 3% interest rate.

- Scenario 2 (Student B)
You are a banker. Your bank is currently offering a 3.5% interest rate. If a customer pays a down payment of at least 20% this can be negotiable, but not dramatically.

8. Grammar Review: Quantifiers

Remind the students that "much" is always followed by an uncountable noun and "many" is followed by countable nouns.
a. How much money would you like to earn?

b. How many projects have you worked on?

c. How much traffic is there is this area?

d. How many courses are you taking this year?

e. How much work do you have to do this week?

f. How many people do think is optimal for a team?

9. Small Group Discussion: Finance

a. What do you think about the stock market?

b. Does the stock market have a good reputation in your country?

c. Do you think stock options are a positive things for companies to offer employees?

d. Do you invest in the stock market? Would you consider doing so in the future? Why or why not?

e. Do you think being a trader is an interesting job? Why or why not?

f. What is the future of the stock market in your opinion?

10. Homework

Tell the students to study the vocabulary related to banking and finance for the next lesson.

11. Vocabulary Bank

Banking vocabulary:
- **Balance**: amount of money in your bank account
- **Branch**: office
- **Checkbook**: book where your checks are
- **Credit card**: card you use to pay for products
- **Current account** = checking account: account you use for daily transactions; linked to your checkbook
- **Savings account**: account where you can put money aside and earn a small percentage of interest
- **Debit**: money removed from your account; debt
- **To deposit**: to put money in your account
- **To withdraw**: to remove money from your account
- **Interest rate**: percentage you have to pay the bank when they grant you a loan
- **Loan**: money given by the bank for a set period of time; you have to reimburse this amount with interest
- **Mortgage**: loan for the purchase of a house
- **Overdraft**: when you spend more than you have in your account
- **Bank statement**: document you receive from your bank at the end of the month showing your debits and credits

Finance vocabulary:
- **Exchange rate**: level of exchange for foreign currency
- **Currency**: money (ie. euro, dollars, yen, etc.)
- **Bear market**: market with falling prices
- **Bull market**: market with rising prices
- **Shares / Stocks**: ownership of part of a company on the stock market
- **Shareholder**: person who owns part of a company on the stock market

- **Stock market**: market where stocks / shares are bought and sold
- **To invest**: to put money into a project with the objective of having a financial return
- **Broker**: agent who buys and sells stock for a commission
- **Trader**: person who buys and sells stocks for a company
- **Dividend**: money paid to shareholders at the end of the year

Chapter 12 – Production

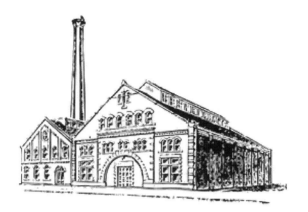

1. Introduction

In this section you will look at:
- Purchasing

- Working on a production line

- R & D

In terms of grammar and vocabulary, you will review:
- The passive

- Vocabulary related to production

2. Review of the Previous Lesson

Go over the banking and finance vocabulary from the previous lesson.

3. Brainstorming: Production

Write "production" on the board. Tell the students they work for a company that manufactures jam. Ask them to tell you what they need in order to produce jam (raw materials: fruit, sugar, citric acid; recipes; machines; workers; jars and packaging, etc.). Go over the process together. Try to elicit the vocabulary for the various steps. (Buy fruit, transport fruit, validate quality of fruit, transfer fruit into factory, wash, sort, cook fruit, add sugar and citric acid, pour in jars, seal lids, put jars on pallets, stock pallets in warehouse...)

4. Grammar Review: Passives (all tenses)

Give the students an active sentence and have them transform it into the passive (example: John buys strawberries in Morocco. – Strawberries are bought in Morocco.)
- John is buying apples in France. (Apples are being bought in France.)

- John bought blueberries in Canada. (Blueberries were bought in Canada.)

- John has bought apricots in Spain. (Apricots have been bought in Spain.)

- John will buy mangoes in Thailand. (Mangoes will be bought in Thailand.)

- John can buy raspberries in Portugal. (Raspberries can be bought in Portugal.)

After they have reviewed this, have them explain the jam-making process using the passive (Buy fruit, transport fruit, validate quality of fruit, transfer fruit into factory, wash, sort, cook fruit, add sugar and citric acid, pour in jars, seal lids, put jars on pallets, stock pallets in warehouse...: The fruit is bought..., It is transported..., The quality of the fruit is validated, etc.)

5. Pair Work: A Process

Once they are clear on the passives, break them into pairs and tell them they are going to present a process to the class.

They can explain how something is manufactured or share a recipe—anything, so long as they use the passive.

Give them 10-15 minutes to prepare and then have each group present their "product" to the rest of the class.

Circulate as they are preparing to see if they need any vocabulary. For groups that have difficulties coming up with an idea, encourage them to explain a common recipe (crepes, chocolate cake, pizza, etc.).

I have also had groups explain how coffee is made, how a piece of furniture is built and how chocolate is made.

6. Group Discussion: Purchasing and R&D

a. What is the role of the purchasing department in the production process?

b. Who do they have to deal with to do their jobs? (suppliers and production team)

c. What kinds of problems can they have? (timing, among other things)

d. What is the role of the R&D Department?

e. How can companies keep their new innovative products secret?

f. What do you think of industrial espionage?

g. What is the role of the production department?

h. What problems can they have?

7. Listening: Producing a New Product

Production (audio files found on the ASAP Coaching video site; see link at the back of the book in the bonus section to have access).

Kyle O'Reilly is the production manager of Jam'Up, a company that produces jam and jellies. He is talking to Heidi Engels, a purchasing assistant, about the production of a new mixed fruit jam that is supposed to start next week.

- We were supposed to receive the blueberries yesterday, but the delivery has been delayed.
- When are they going to get here?
- I hope the day after tomorrow, but the transport company is on strike, so there's no guarantee.
- We need them in five days, at the latest, if we are going to begin production on time.
- If you have everything else ready and you only have to wash and sort the blueberries, what is your absolute latest deadline?
- You just heard it. We can prepare the raspberries, blackberries and currants between now and Thursday, but we have to have the blueberries by then."
- There is a possible alternative.
- If you are talking about using the frozen blueberries, forget it. This is supposed to be a 'super fresh recipe—quality guaranteed'. The marketing department will have a fit if they have to change the labels. Frozen berries don't meet the super fresh guarantee.
- I know that, but don't you think having some jam as opposed to no jam for the launch is a better option?
- Don't take it out on me! I am just telling you what Susan in marketing will tell you.

- I know. Sorry, Kyle. Let's just hope the blueberries get here on time so we don't have to figure out a plan B.

8. R & D Discussion

a. Talk about an innovative product that impresses you. Why does it impress you?

b. How important is innovation in company growth?

c. How do people in the R&D department find new ideas?

d. Would you like to work in R&D? Why or why not?

9. Small Group Presentation: Innovation

Break the class into small groups. Have them brainstorm things they would like to improve in their everyday life – for example, at home, at school, in the local community...

Tell them they need to choose one of these problems and brainstorm ways to improve or solve it. It could be a new product, invention or idea for a new way of doing things or for adapting an existing product.

Each group must prepare and give a presentation (with PowerPoint) of their idea to the class:
Instructions for the presentation:
- Open the presentation

- Show a simple design of the new product/idea

- Explain why it is the best idea

- Describe your target market and explain how you would promote your product (Give at least one example of a commercial, a print ad, a radio ad....)

- Close the presentation and answer any questions

Your presentation must be about 15 minutes long and each person in your group must speak an equal amount.

The students can begin the brainstorming section of this assignment during class time. After that, you can select dates for them to do their presentations in front of the class.

10. Homework

Tell the students to study the vocabulary related to purchasing, production and R&D for the next lesson. They also need to prepare their innovation presentations.

11. Vocabulary Bank

Purchasing vocabulary:
- **Acquisition**: the act of obtaining something
- **Bill of lading**: document issued by a carrier to a shipper that specifies the terms of delivery
- **Incoterms**: terms used for international shipment of goods
- **Commodity**: article of trade or commerce
- **Delivery**: the act of distributing merchandise
- **Goods**: merchandise
- **Invoice**: a list of goods purchased or services provided, including all costs
- **Lead time**: time is takes a supplier to deliver merchandise after order is confirmed
- **Net price**: final price
- **Purchase order**: commercial document to place an order for a certain number of products in exchange for a certain price
- **Call for tender** = request for proposal:
- **Sales tax** = VAT: tax consumers pay on retail products, collected by the retailer and paid to the government
- **Warranty**: guarantee for a product

Production vocabulary
- **Automation**: automatic operation and/or control of machines or equipment
- **To manufacture**: to produce a product
- **Defect**: when there is a problem with a product
- **Factory**: building where goods are produced
- **Packaging**: wrapping around a product
- **Plant manager**: person responsible for factory
- **Production manager**: person responsible for production in a factory
- **Line worker**: worker who works on production line

- **Logistics**: planning and coordination of operations in a company (ie. stock, shipping, etc.)
- **Label**: paper on a product with the name of the product, ingredients, etc.
- **Quality control**: verification of the quality of a product
- **Safety**: means to protect against danger of accidents (The staff wears safety equipment.)
- **Security**: means to protect against intentional attack like crime or sabotage (A security guard protects the factory.)
- **Output**: amount or quantity produced during a given time
- **Stock level / Inventory**: amount of stock available
- **Warehouse**: building where products are stocked
- **Storage**: where raw materials are stocked

R&D vocabulary:
- **To innovate**: to introduce an idea or product for the first time
- **Innovation**: introduction of new methods, ideas
- **Industrial espionage**: when competitors steal commercial or technical information
- **Sample**: a small section of a whole, used to make comparisons
- **Test**: trial to evaluate something

BONUS

BONUS 1 - The (only) 50 Irregular Verbs you need to know

There are a lot of irregular verbs, and unfortunately there is no trick to learning them. They have to be memorized. The good news is, you won't use half the verbs on the list as quite a few of them are rather obscure.

I have split the verbs I think are important into four main categories to make memorization a little easier. There may be some that you consider important that I have not included on the list.

The four categories are: Money, Daily Life, Work and Holidays.

Oh, and ok, there's a little more than 50 verbs. If you really want to stick to 50 then only use the first 3 categories and forget about Holidays. But really, who wants to forget about holidays?

Money
Bet, bet, bet (You bet money when you play poker.)
Buy, bought, bought (You buy things when you go shopping.)
cost, cost, cost (A Ferrari costs a lot.)
lend, lent, lent (The bank lends you money.)
lose, lost, lost (You lose money.)
make, made, made (You make money.)
overdraw, overdrew, overdrawn (If you spend more than you have in your bank account, you are overdrawn.)
pay, paid, paid (I paid a lot for my house.)
sell, sold, sold (The Gap sells clothes.)
spend, spent, spent (I spent a lot of money during the sales.)
steal, stole, stolen (Someone stole my wallet with all my money in it!)
win, won, won (I won 10 million euros in the lottery.)

Daily Life

be, was/were, been (I was at work yesterday.)
begin, began, begun (I began working at 9am.)
come, came, come (I came home from work at 6pm.)
do, did, done (My children do their homework.)
drink, drank, drunk (I drink coffee in the morning.)
eat, ate, eaten (We eat breakfast together.)
feed, fed, fed (I feed the cat and then I feed my children dinner.)
get, got, got (I got a letter in the mail today.)
give, gave, given (My daughter gave me a kiss.)
go, went, gone (My children go to school at 8am.)
have, had, had (I had car problems on my way to work.)
leave, left, left (My husband left the office at 7pm.)
read, read (pron. red*), read* (I read with my children before bed.)
see, saw, seen (I saw my daughter's teacher at school.)
sleep, slept, slept (We sleep in late on weekends.)
speak, spoke, spoken (I spoke to my husband before bed.)
take, took, taken (I take a shower in the morning.)
wake, woke, woken (I wake up at 6.)
wear, wore, worn (My daughter wore jeans to school yesterday.)
write, wrote, written (I wrote a note to my husband before I went to work.)

Work

beat, beat, beaten (It's important to beat the competition.)
break, broke, broken (You mustn't break your contract.)
build, built, built (He build his company from the ground up.)
choose, chose, chosen (We chose the best candidate for the job.)
cut, cut, cut (He cut all the employees' salaries after the financial crisis started.)
deal, dealt, dealt (We deal with problems every day.)
drive, drove, driven (I drive to work.)

forecast, forecast/forecasted, forecast/forecasted (The accountant forecast a good year for us next year.)
get, got, got (I got a promotion.)
hold, held, held (We held a meeting to discuss the problem.)
know, knew, known (I know my colleagues very well.)
learn, learned/learnt, learned/learnt (We learned how to use the new IT system.)
quit, quit, quit (Michael quit his job.)
run, ran, run (I run all day long at work!)
say, said, said (My boss said that we need to discuss the issue.)
show, showed, shown (The architect showed us the plans.)
teach, taught, taught (The trainer taught us how to use the new IT system.)
tell, told, told (My boss told us about the pay cuts during our yearly appraisals.)
understand, understood, understood (I understand all the nuances of my job.)

Holidays
catch, caught, caught (I caught the frisbee on the beach.)
dive, dived/dove, dived (I dove with sharks in Australia.)
fall, fell, fallen (We fell in love with Corsica during our holidays.)
fell, felt, felt (I never feel more relaxed than during my holidays.)
find, found, found (My daughter found a starfish on the beach.)
fly, flew, flown (We flew to Thailand for our last holidays.)
forget, forgot, forgotten (You forget all your problems when you are on holiday.)
let, let, let (We let our children stay up late during the holidays.)
meet, met, met (We met some very nice people in Cambodia.)
put, put, put (We put our towels on the beach.)
ride, rode, ridden (She rode a bicycle around the island.)
send, sent, sent (I sent postcards to my family.)
sing, sang, sung (We sang songs in the car on our way to Marseilles.)
sit, sat, sat (We sat in traffic for hours!)

stand, stood, stood (And then we stood in a long queue to visit the Louvre.)
swim, swam, swum (I swam in the Pacific Ocean.)
think, thought, thought (We didn't think about work at all.)
throw, threw, thrown (My children threw a ball on the beach.)

BONUS 2 - The Audio files

You want to be sure about the pronunciation ? The dialogs in this book have been recorded and are available on our website:

http://www.asap-videos.com/eslft

or simply scan the following bar code:

Enjoy...

BONUS 3 - The TOP20 idiomatic expressions

In parenthesis, the definition of the expression (even if in most cases, they are clear enough !).

- No pain, no gain (i.e. there's no reward without effort)
- Talkers are not doers (Those who talk the most are not the ones who act the most)
- Better late than never (about something or someone that arrives late...)
- When pigs fly! (about something that will never happen)
- That drives me crazy! (about an issue that's pretty annoying)
- It's getting on my nerves (same one but a little less annoying)
- So much for that (about something we thought big and which eventually ends up small...)
- Leave nothing to chance (means everything has to be prepared, calculated...)
- Between a rock and a hard place (about a situation where both choices are tough)
- All that glitters is not gold (about something which seems great but is actually not)
- I could eat a horse (when you are very hungry !)
- It's none of your business (pretty clear indeed !)
- To kill two birds with one stone (to execute two operations with the same movement)
- It's raining cats and dogs (when it rains *a lot*)
- It costs an arm and a leg (about something very expensive)
- It was a piece of cake (about something very easy)
- It's as easy as a pie (same thing, about something very easy)
- It's crystal clear (when something is understood perfectly)
- A little bird told me... (when you get a piece of information in an unofficial way)
- No news is good news (what you hope when you are expecting news that doesn't arrive)

- Where there's a will there's a way (used to mean that if you are determined enough, you can find a way to achieve what you want, even if it is very difficult)

BONUS 4 - The Special Amazon bonus

We've reserved a special bonus for Amazon readers; it's a **great** offer for our other books, **Business English in 5 minutes, Speak fluent English** (like a native) and **Fuel for lively conversations in English**:

Business English in 5 minutes, Speak Fluent English and **Fuel for lively conversations in English** are excellent add-ons to ESL for Teachers and will definitely refine your English skills.

And you can actually get one of them for free!

Please find what it's all about here on this private page of our website:

http://www.asap-videos.com/amazon-bonus

Made in the USA
San Bernardino, CA
17 March 2019